Louis Armstrong

Paul Revere

de Jones

Tow Truck Letters:

Magic C

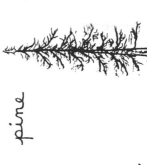

pine

Cursive Success

#4494 0293

by Jan Z. Olsen, O.T.R.

Developer of the Handwriting Without Tears™ curriculum

Author of My Printing Book, Printing Power, and Cursive Handwriting

helicopter

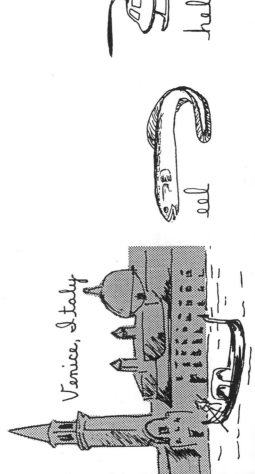

Venice, Italy

Handwriting Without Tears™
Jan Z. Olsen, O.T.R.

8802 Quiet Stream Court
Potomac, MD 20854
phone: 301-983-8409   fax: 301-983-6821
www.hwtears.com   Jan@hwtears.com

Copyright © 1999 Jan Z. Olsen
Second Edition
ISBN: 1-891627-11-2
123456789AGS0099

Table of Contents

Dear Students,

I wrote this book to help you learn an easy and neat way to write in cursive. After you learn the basics in this book, you'll gradually evolve your own personal style. Practice slowly and your speed will develop. Have fun and enjoy the book.

Jan Z. Olsen

Dear Teachers and Parents,

Welcome to Handwriting Without Tears™! I'm Jan Olsen, OTR, the developer of the program. I'm an occupational therapist and have specialized in handwriting for the last 23 years. Handwriting Without Tears™ is the culmination of my work. It is a developmentally based method that makes printing and cursive easy.

My interest in handwriting came from helping my own son, who had printing problems in the first grade. Since that time in the mid - 1970s, I have worked with thousands of children, parents, teachers and therapists to help them learn the sensible and compelling aspects of the Handwriting Without Tears™ program.

Today, parents, teachers and therapists can use my materials and methods to insure handwriting success for their children. The Handwriting Without Tears™ curriculum is a comprehensive program. It teaches writing readiness skills, printing and cursive. It is as easy and enjoyable for parents and teachers as it is for children.

The purpose of my work is to make handwriting available to children as an automatic, natural skill. Students who write well and easily, do better in school, enjoy their classes more and feel proud of themselves. The Handwriting Without Tears™ method can help you make this difference for your students.

Introduction

Cursive Success is the advanced student workbook for cursive. It follows the beginning student workbook, Cursive Handwriting. Students in higher grades may begin with Cursive Success. Both workbooks use a clean, clear, vertical style that is very easy to read and write. Students enjoy the short, simple lessons.

Cursive Success reviews the formation of lower-case cursive letters. It has step – by – step illustrations and memorable teaching tips.

Strong emphasis is placed on connecting letters into words. Students use the special "Review and Mastery" pages to develop a natural fluency in cursive writing.

You will notice the Handwriting Without Tears™ double lines. A large size is used to teach new letters, middle size for word practice and small size for mastery.

Use the Cursive Teacher's Guide with this workbook. The teaching strategies will help you be an active and successful handwriting teacher. I wish you success in helping your children learn to write fluently and well.

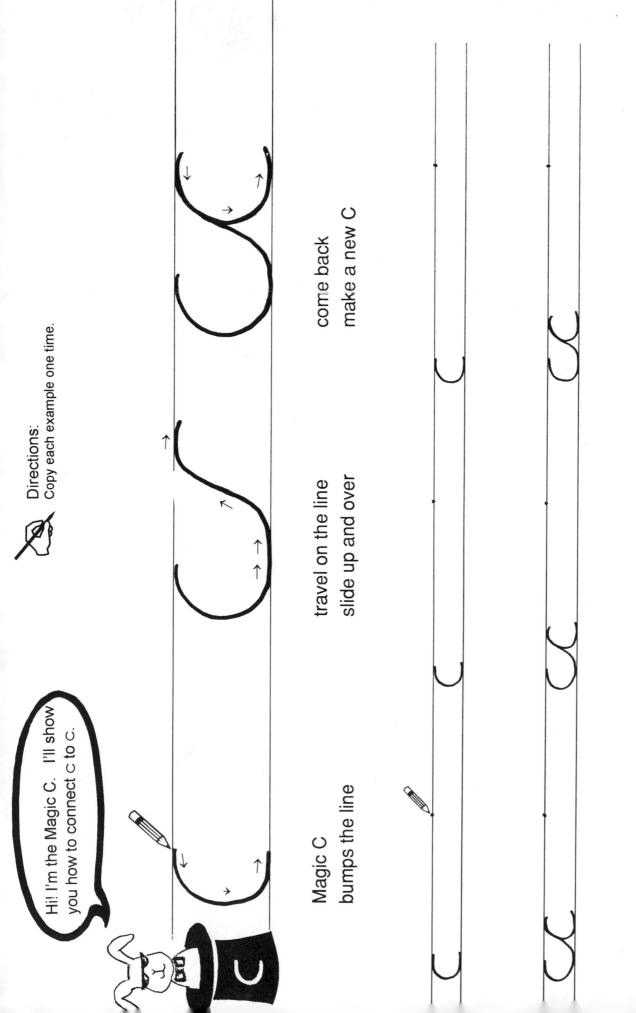

Change c into a. Here's how-

Magic C
bumps the line

up
like a

bump

back down
bump
travel away

Tip - Travel on the line between letters.
(move your pencil on the bottom line before you begin the next letter)

a

ac

aa

Directions:
Copy each example one time.

Cursive Warm-up:　　Start at *　　draw a line under U and over O　　stop at *

U O　　*U O*　　*U O*　　*U O*　　*U O*

5

Now change c into d.

Magic C

up
like a

up higher

slide down
bump
travel away

d   d   d

d   d

d   d

aaa   aaa   dad

aaa   aaa   dad

dad   dad   dad

d

dc

da

cd

ad

cad

add

dad

7

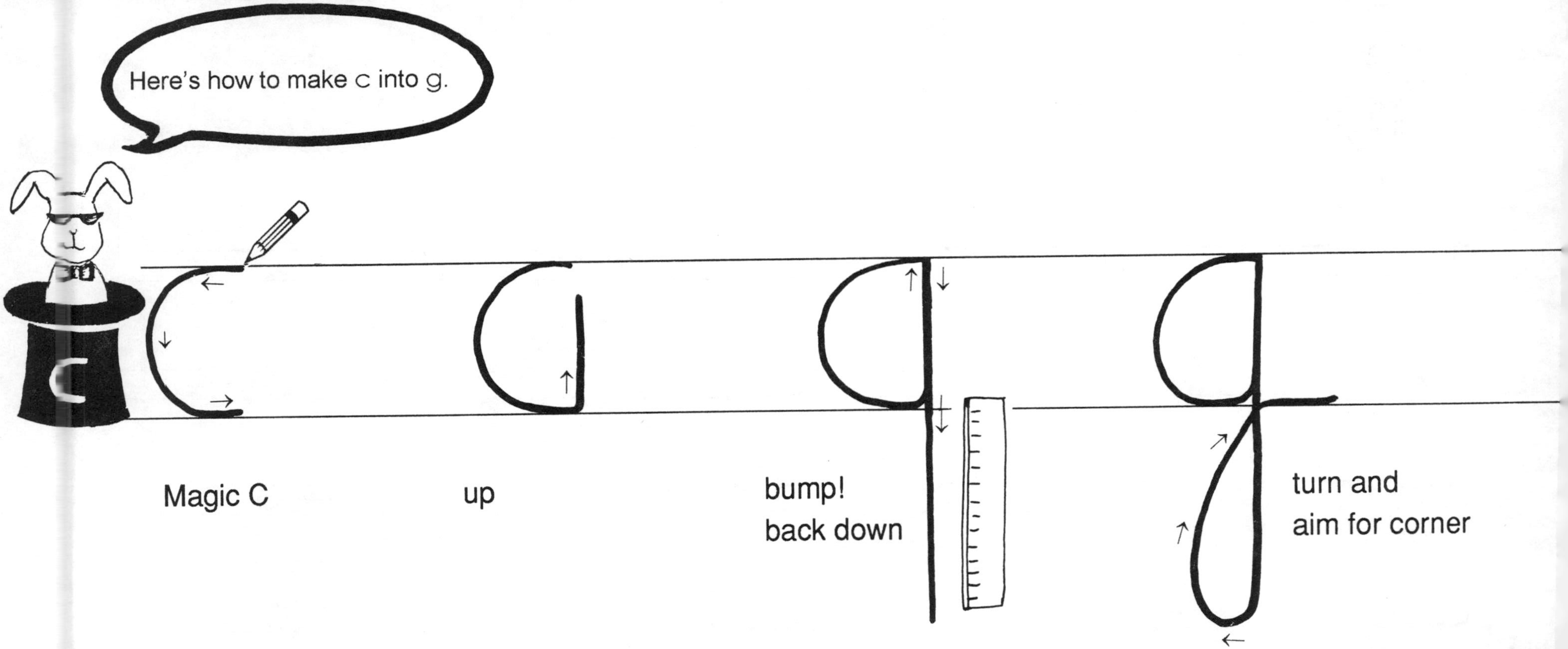

Here's how to make c into g.

Magic C

up

bump!
back down

turn and
aim for corner

gad

gad

gad

gad

8

Make the line as straight as a ruler.

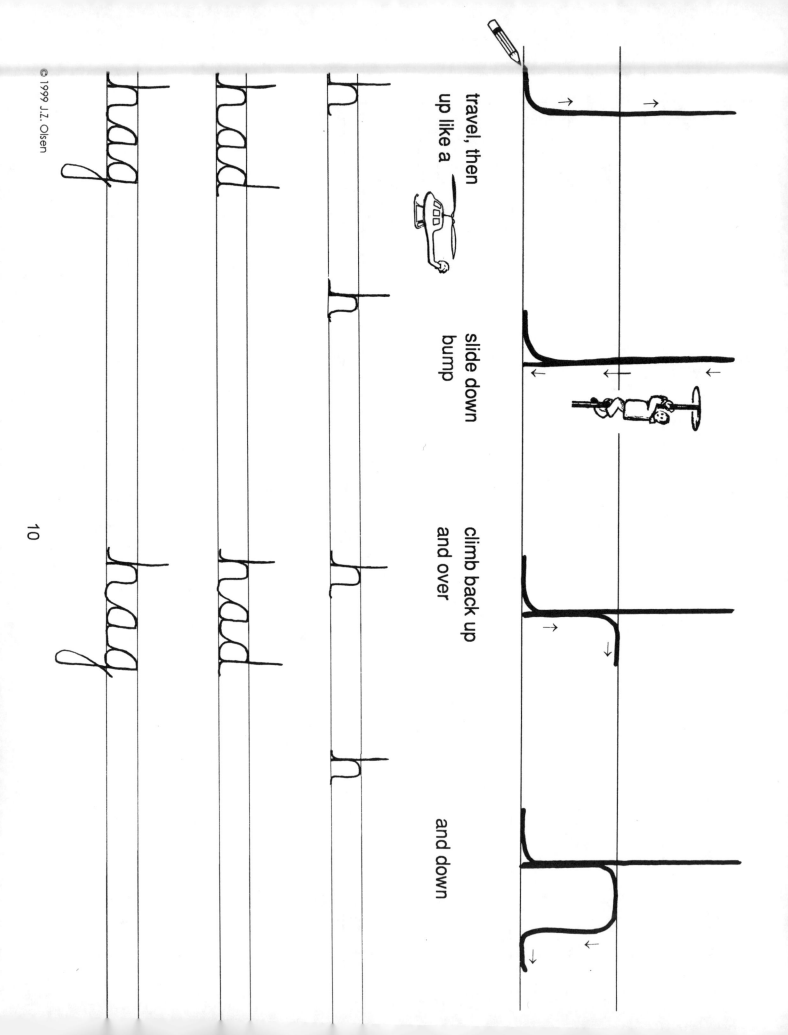

travel, then
up like a

slide down
bump

climb back up
and over

and down

10

11

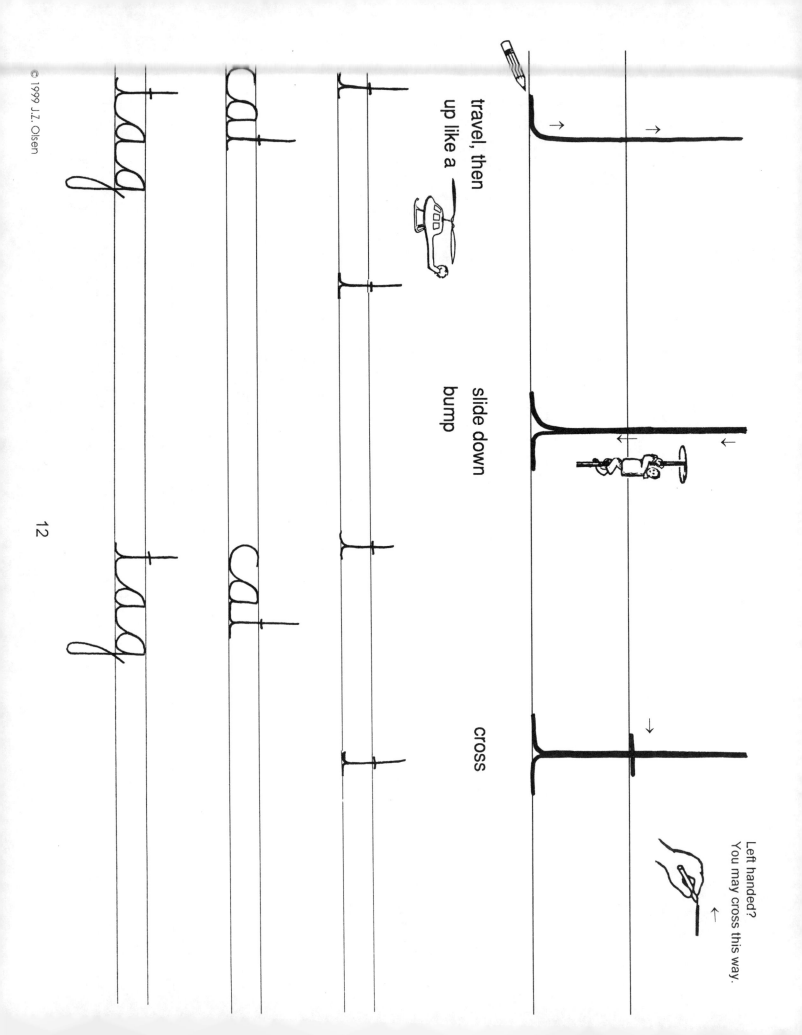

travel, then up like a

slide down

cross

bump

Left handed?
You may cross this way.

cat

cat

tag

tag

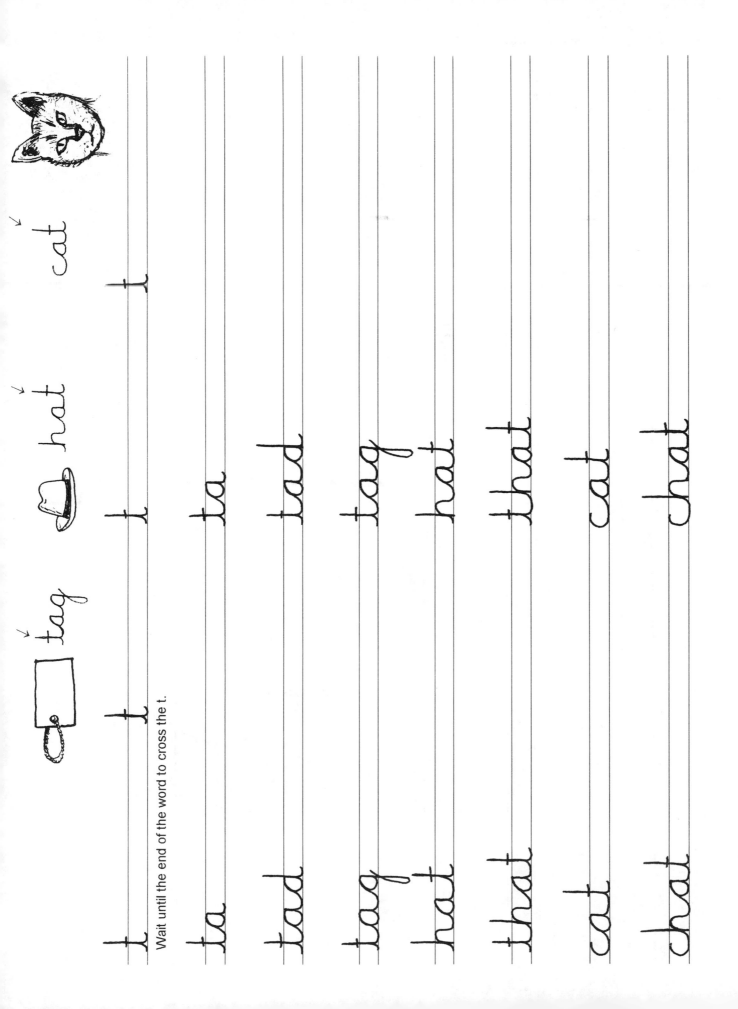

tag

hat

cat

Wait until the end of the word to cross the t.

t

ta

tad

tag

hat

that

cat

that

13

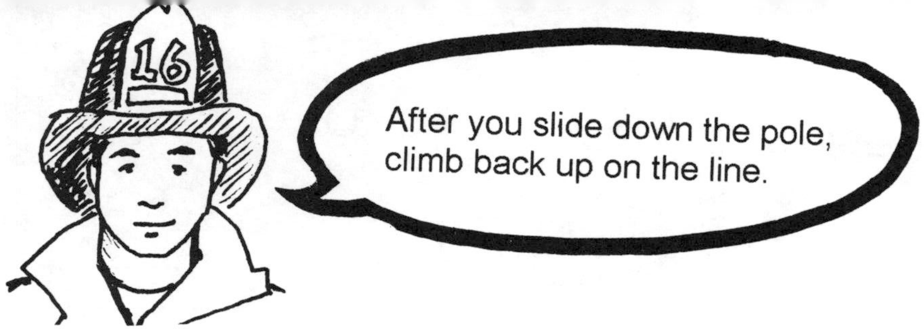

After you slide down the pole, climb back up on the line.

travel,
up like a

slide down

climb back up
bump
over + around

bump the pole
travel away

P   P   P

P   P   P

pat

pat

cap

p   p   p

pac   pac

pad   pad

gap   gap

cap   cap

pa   pa

pat   pat

path   path

15

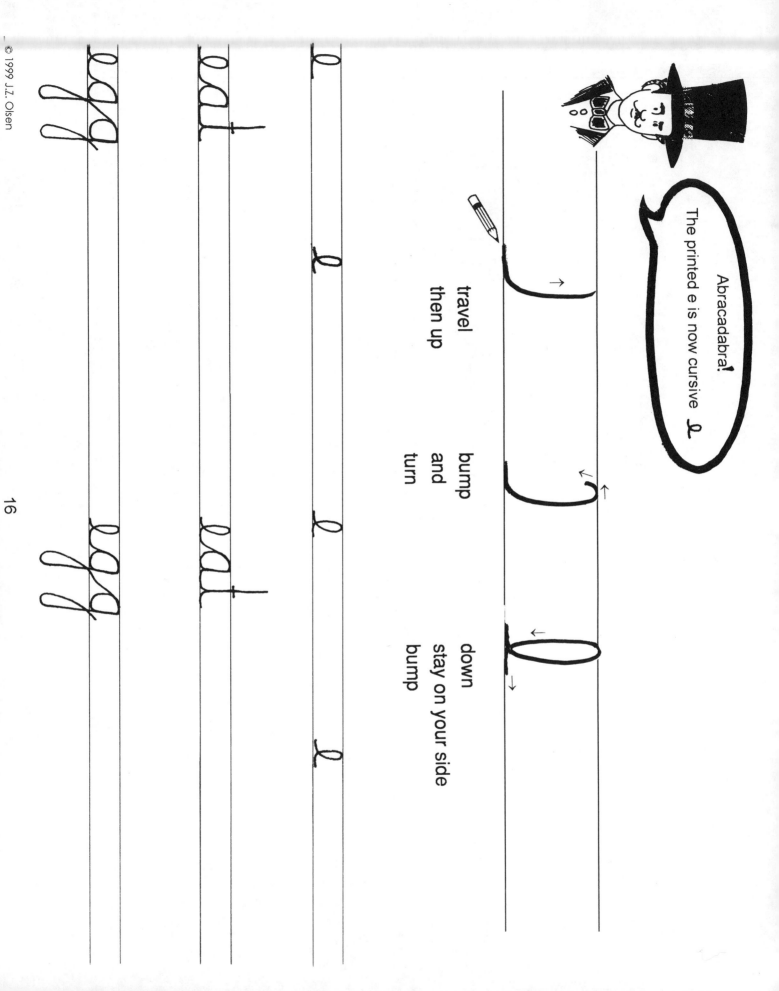

Abracadabra!
The printed e is now cursive ℓ

travel
then up

bump
and
turn

down
stay on your side
bump

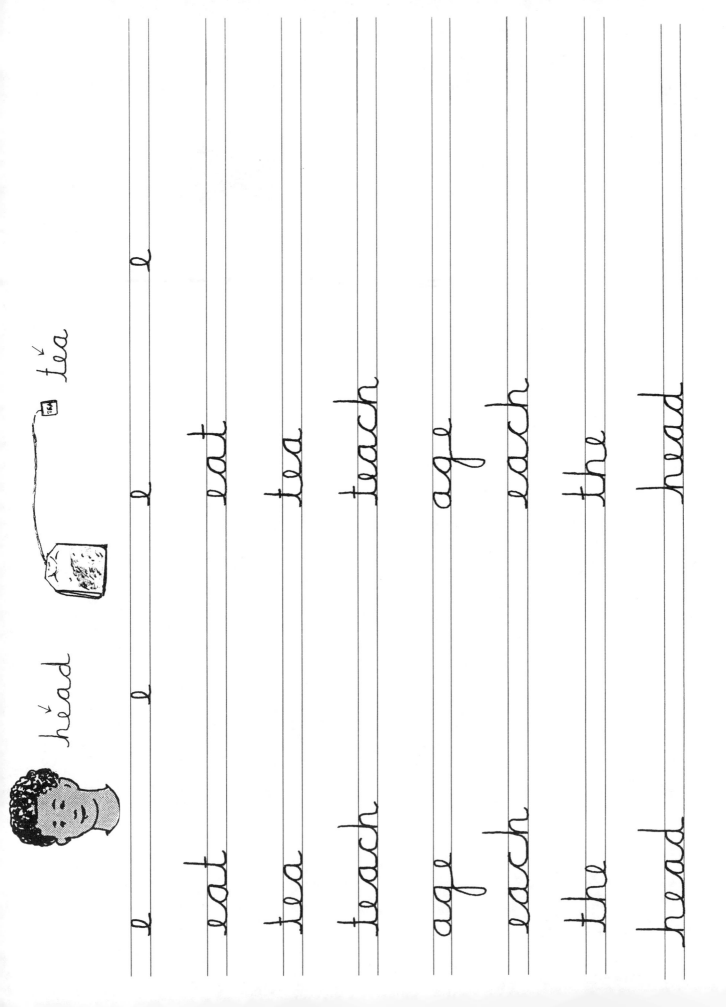

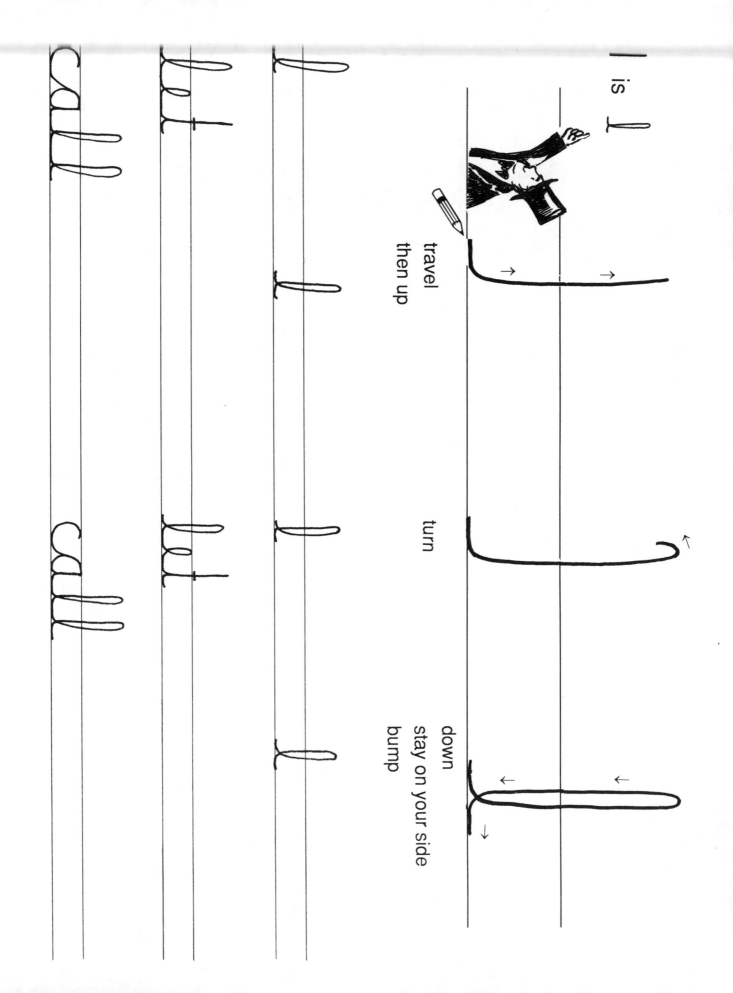

is L

travel
then up

turn

down
stay on your side
bump

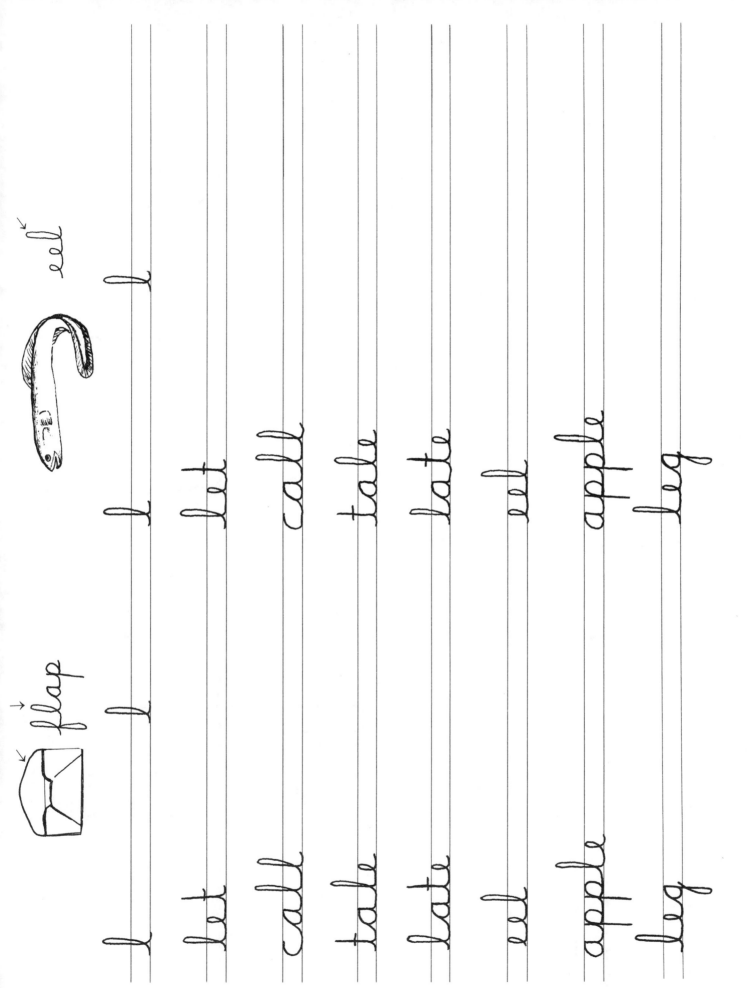

eel

flap

l   l   l

let   l

call   let

tale   call

late   tale

eel   late

apple   eel

leg   apple

leg

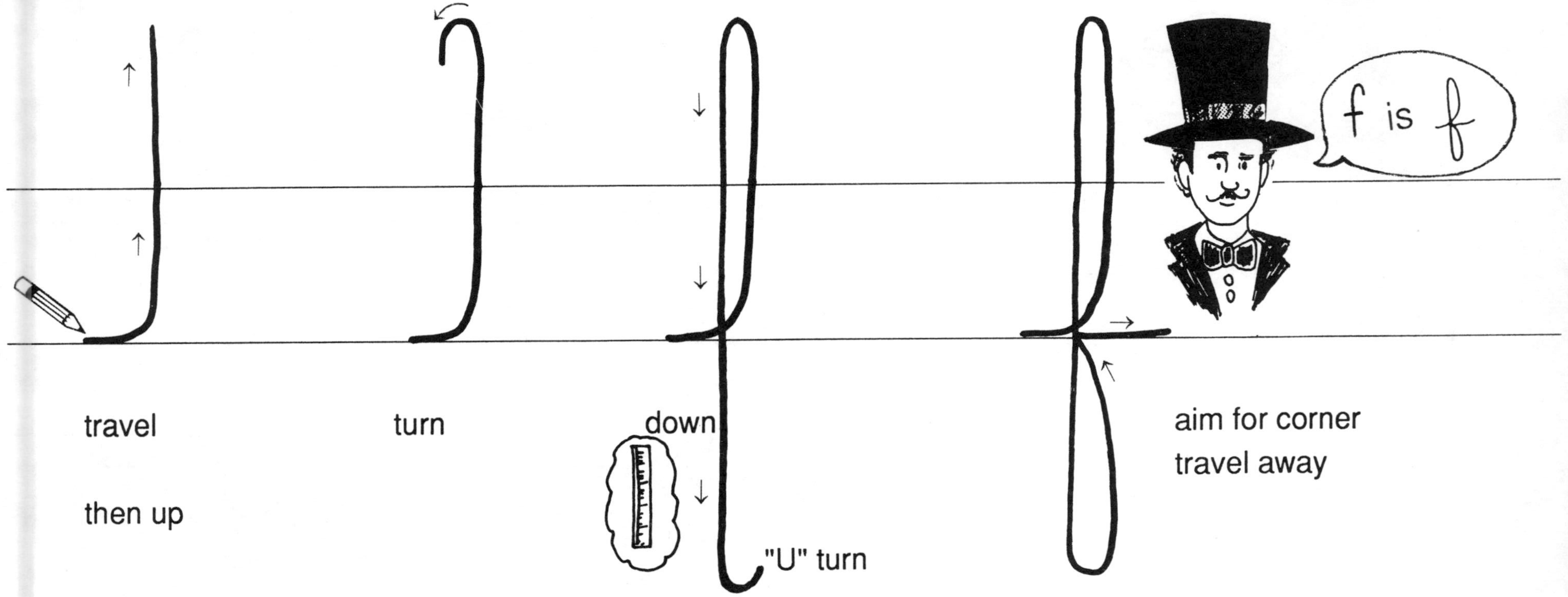

travel

then up

turn

down

"U" turn

Tip - Make the line as straight as a ruler.

aim for corner
travel away

f is ƒ

calf

feet

calf

feet

face

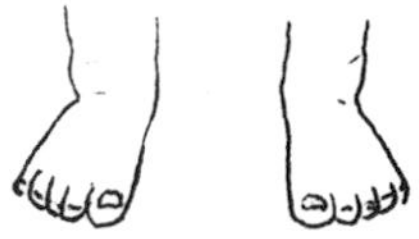

feet

f

f

f

face

feet

calf

fed

act

fact

flap

face

feet

calf

fed

act

fact

flap

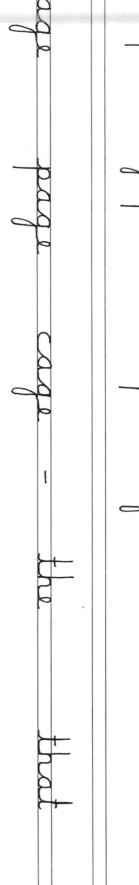

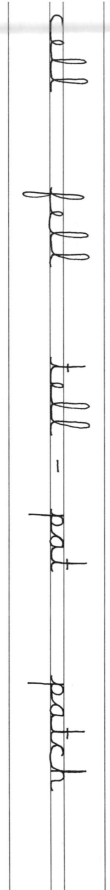

a c d e f g h   l

had   pad   dad — ate   date   late

cap   gap   tap — fall   tall   call

age   page   cage — the   that

call   fall   tall — pat   patch

DIRECTIONS:
1. Do your best.
2. Copy each word group once. (You may skip around.)
3. Take your time. There is no hurry.

REVIEW AND MASTERY PAGES WILL HELP YOUR:
1. Memory - You will really master these 10 letters!
2. Size – You'll learn to use a smaller size.
3. Fluency - The repeated letter patterns (had, pad, fad) will help your cursive flow naturally.

Review and Mastery

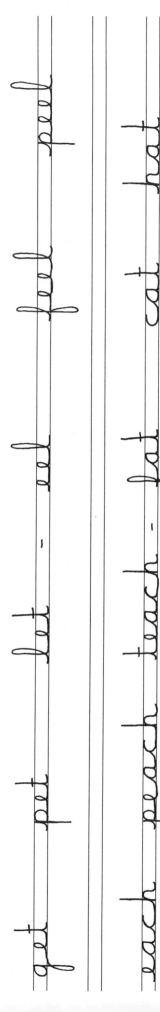
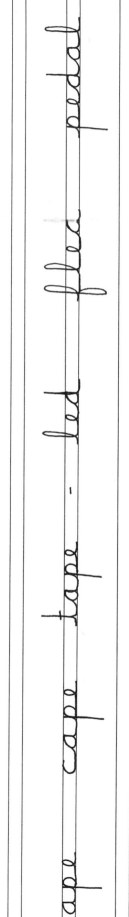

MORE REVIEW – "TRANSLATE" PRINT TO CURSIVE
a c d e f g h l p t

1. Print these letters at the top of a piece of paper.
2. Print words using only these 10 letters.
3. Now "translate" the words into cursive.

TOTAL MASTERY – THE "SILLY SPELLING" TEST
a c d e f g h l p t

1. Number your paper.
2. The teacher will call out the words and spell them!
3. You write the words in cursive.

23

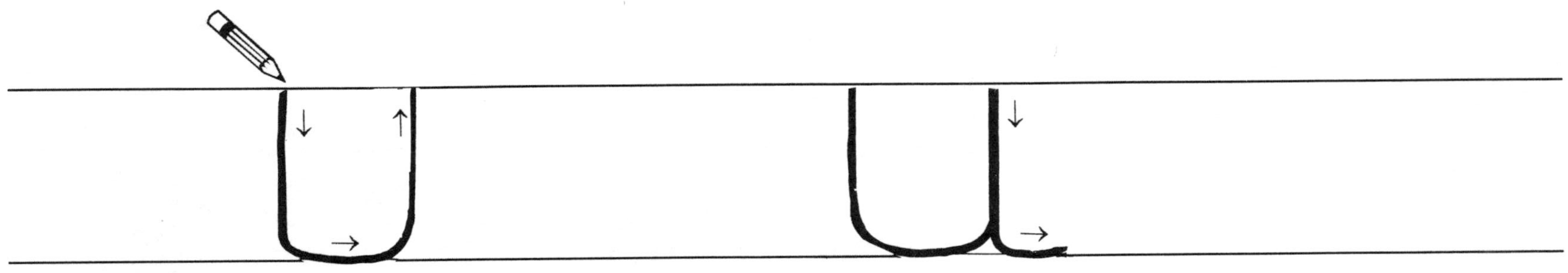

down
travel
up, bump

slide down
travel

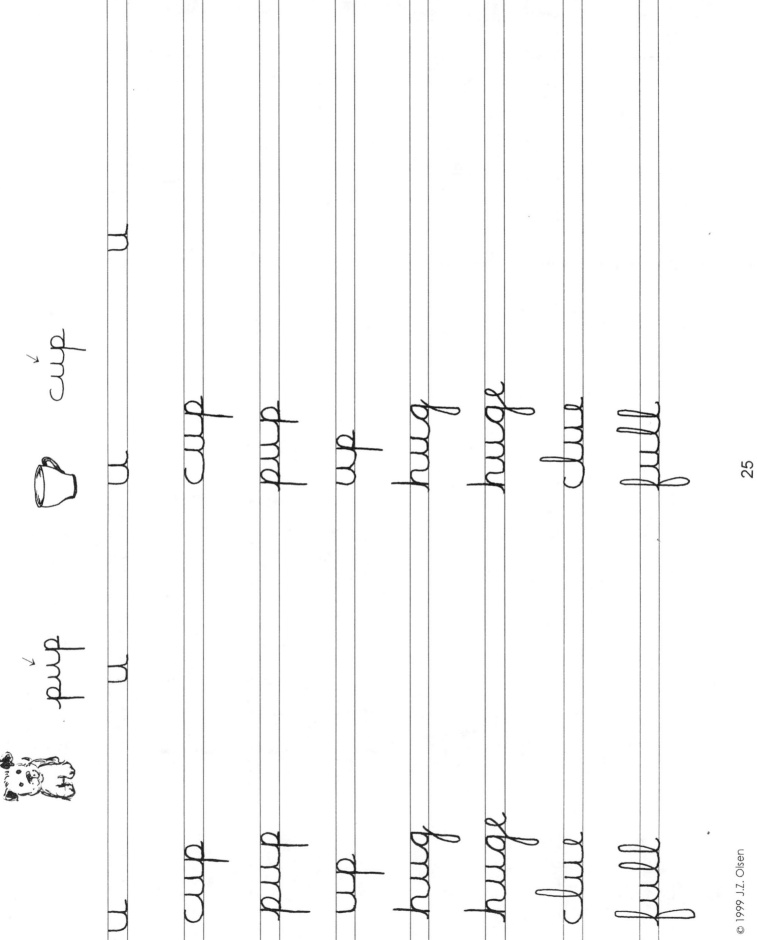

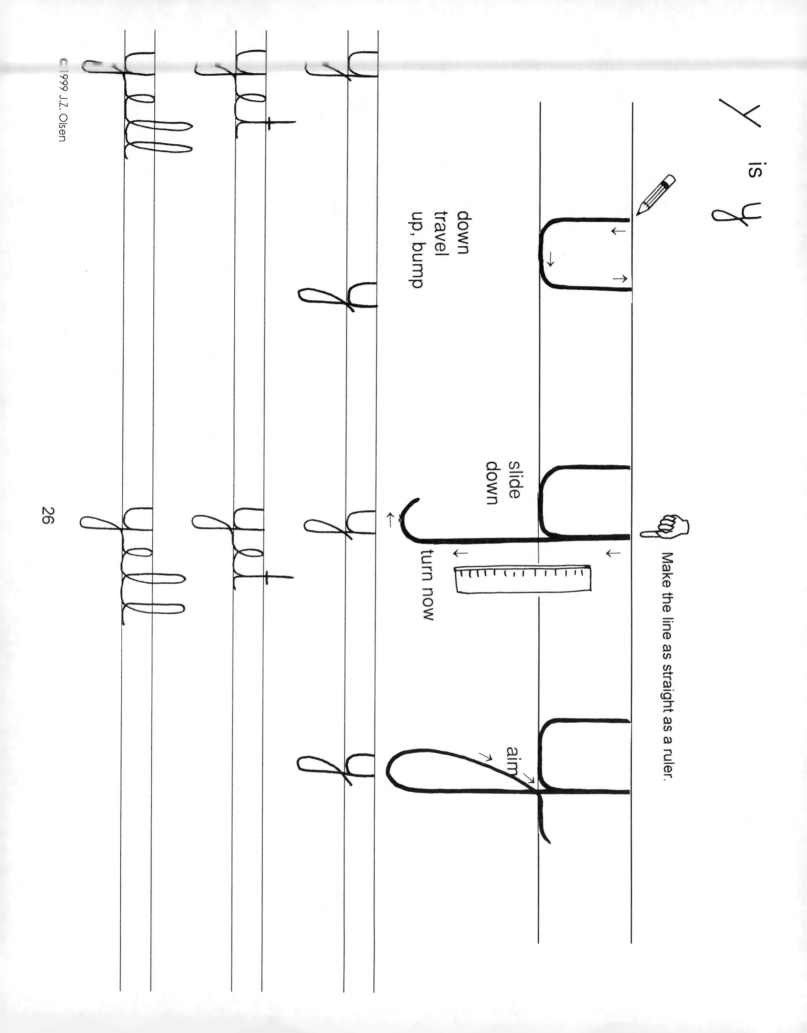

Y is y

down
travel
up, bump

slide
down

turn now

aim

Make the line as straight as a ruler.

26

Seeing spots?
No, these are dots.

travel
up
bump

down
bump
travel

dot!

dig

ice

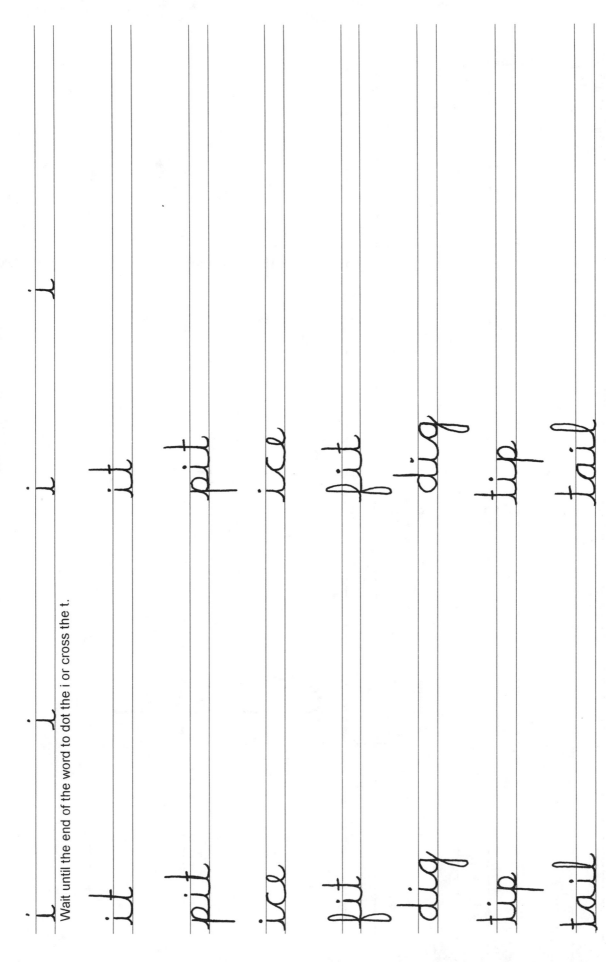

tail

i   i   i

Wait until the end of the word to dot the i or cross the t.

it

pit

ice

fit

dig

tip

tail

29

Seeing spots?
No, these are dots.

j   is   ⌡

travel
up

down
turn

aim

travel
dot!

jay

juicy

Wait until the end of the word to dot the j.

jet

judge

joy

juggle

jeep

juicy

Review and Mastery

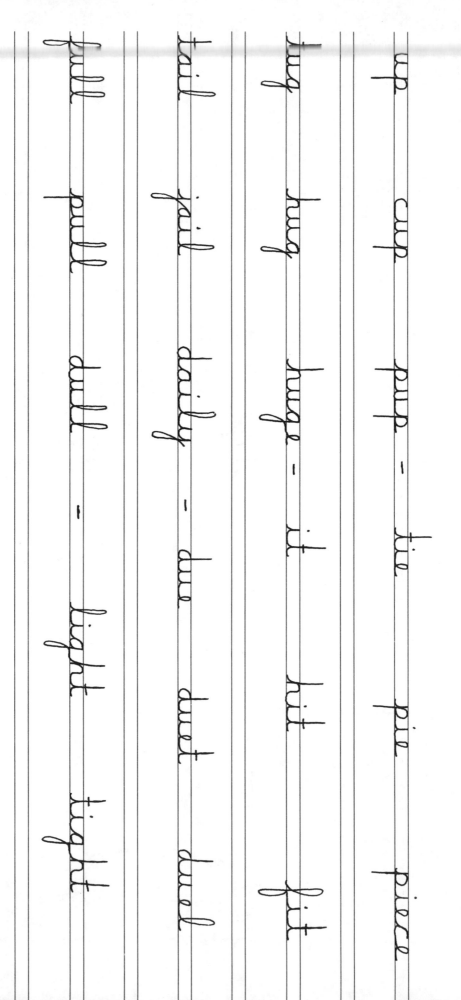

a c d e f g h i j l

up — cup — tie — pie — piece

tug — hug — huge — it — hit — fit

tail — jail — daily — due — duet — duel

full — pull — dull — light — light

MORE REVIEW – "TRANSLATE" PRINT TO CURSIVE

a c d e f g h i j l p t u y

1. Print these letters at the top of a piece of paper.
2. Print words using only these 14 letters.
3. Now "translate" the words into cursive.

Review and Mastery

p t u y

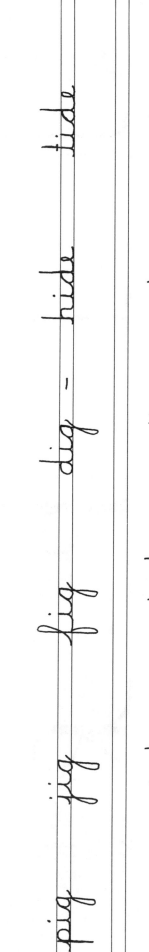

pig jig dig hide tide

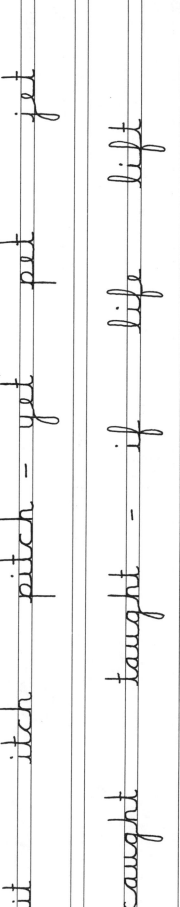

it itch pitch yet pot get

caught if life lift

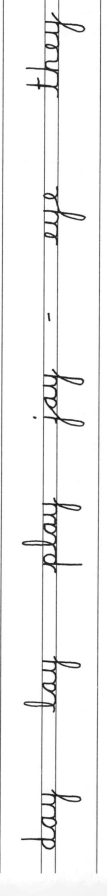

day play jay eye they

TOTAL MASTERY – THE "SILLY SPELLING" TEST
a c d e f g h i j l p t u y

1. Number your paper.
2. The teacher will call out the words and spell them!
3. You write the words in cursive.

33

k is k

travel +
up

down
bump

up
over
around

kick!
slide away

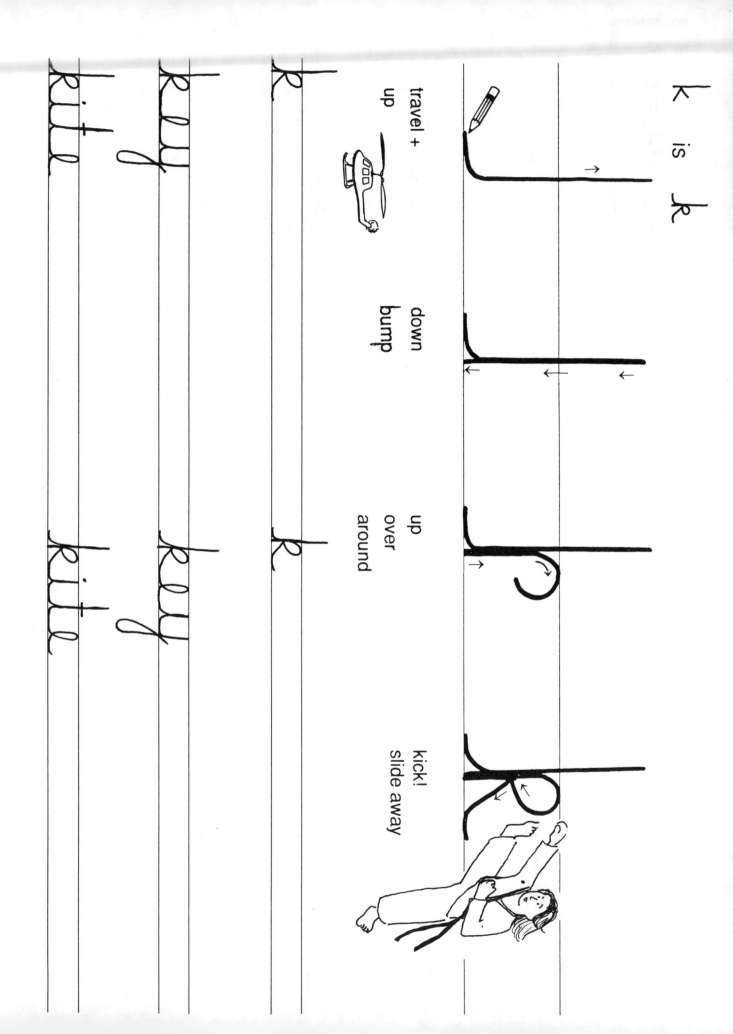

34

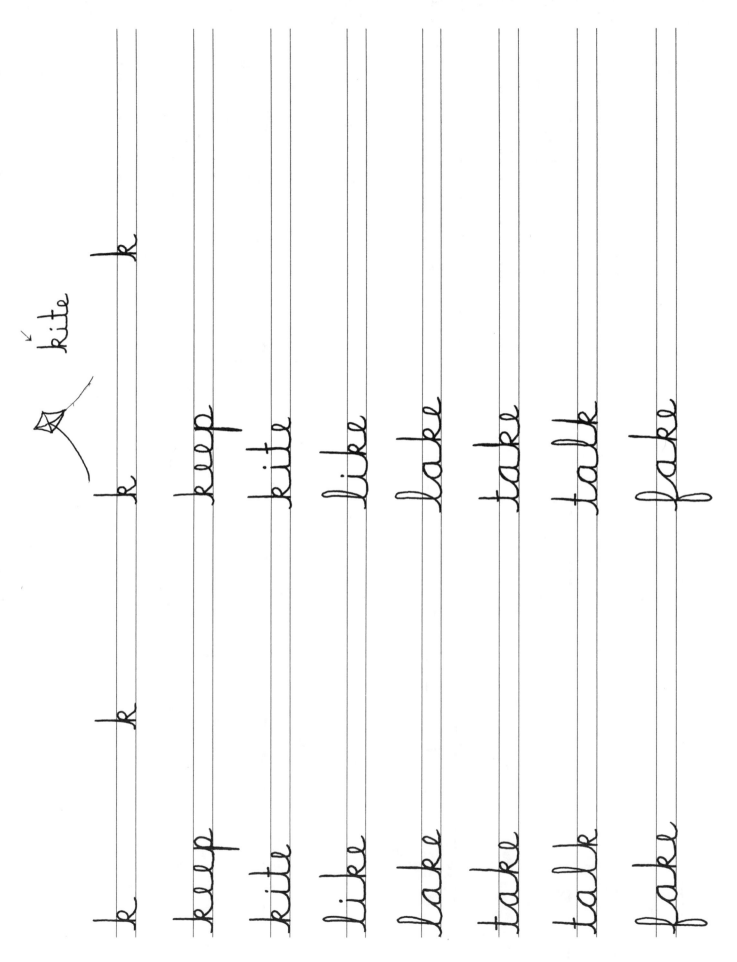

k   k   k

kite

keep   keep   keep

kite   kite   kite

like   like   like

lake   lake   lake

take   take   take

talk   talk   talk

fake   fake   fake

35

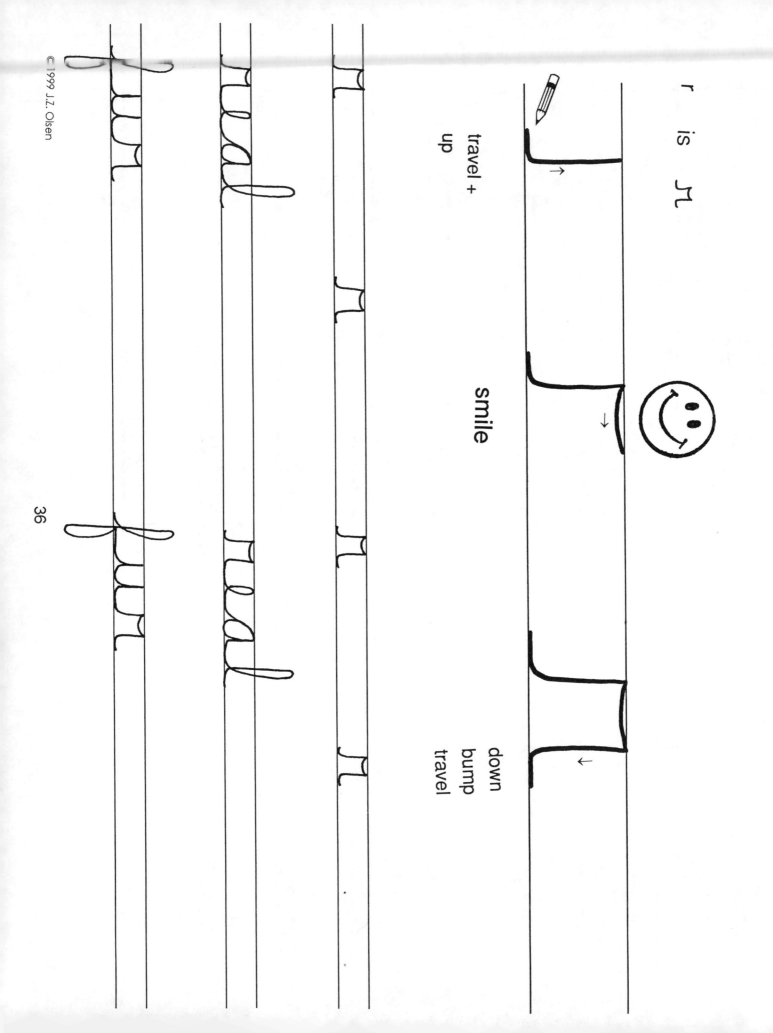

r is ⌐

travel + up

smile

down
bump
travel

rake

r

r   r

race   race

can   can

fan   fan

rake   rake

are   are

after   after

raft   raft

37

s is a

straight jet take-off
bump
stop!

bump!

make a J
drop

touch
sneak away

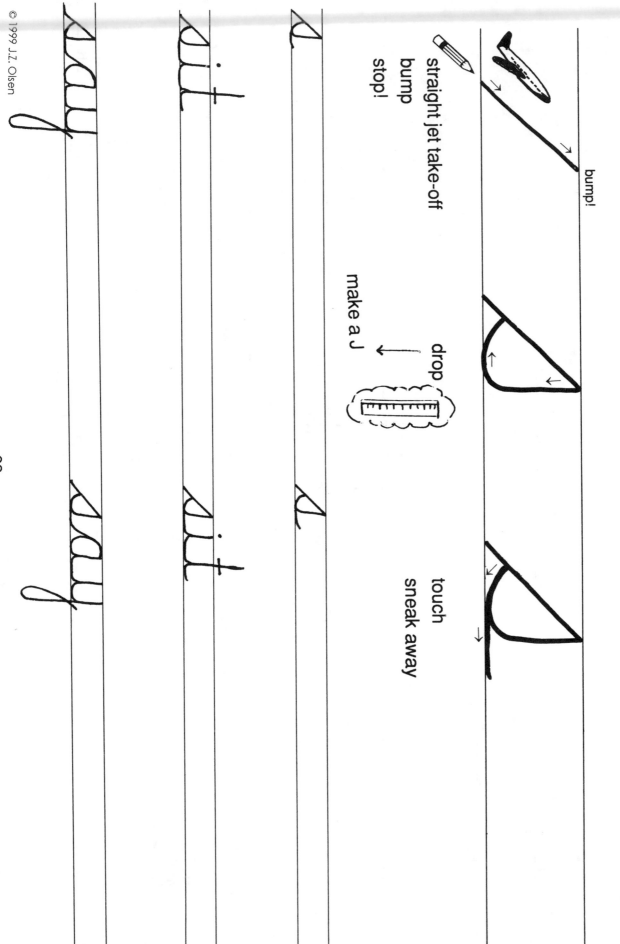

salt

s　s　s

salt

sell

self

say

yes

it

sit

supper

39

a c d e f g h i j k l

slice   juice – yes   yesterday.

keep   deep – race   face   place

read   real   reach – put   hut   duty

quit   quat – fire   tire   tired

MORE REVIEW – "TRANSLATE" PRINT TO CURSIVE

a c d e f g h i j k l p r s t u y

1. Print these letters at the top of a piece of paper.
2. Print words using only these 17 letters.
3. Now "translate" the words into cursive.

p r s t u y f

side ride decide - cry try fry

sick lick pick - ear hear fear

car card hard - use useful us

ate skate late - jet jetty jolly

TOTAL MASTERY – THE "SILLY SPELLING" TEST

a c d e f g h i j k l p r s t u y

1. Number your paper.
2. The teacher will call out the words and spell them!
3. You write the words in cursive.

41

Now you are ready to learn the tow truck letters.

They tow letters by joining them up at the "hook."

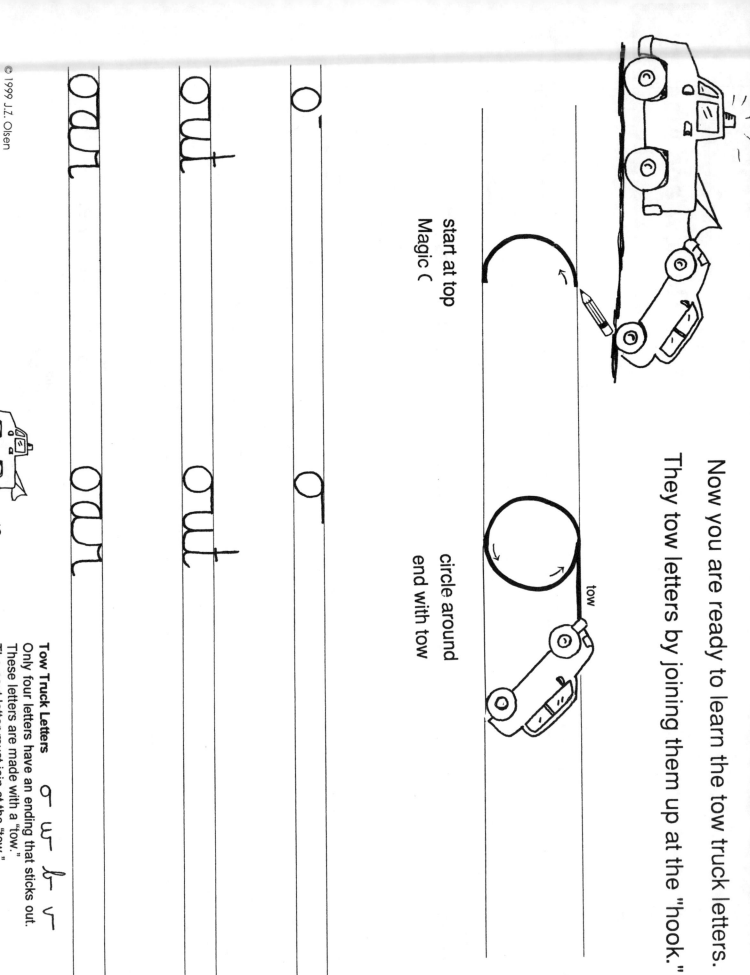

tow

start at top
Magic C

circle around
end with tow

o

o

out

out

out

out

Tow Truck Letters o w b v

Only four letters have an ending that sticks out.

These letters are made with a "tow."

The next letter must join at the "tow."

For now, always make a "straight across tow."

Now you are ready to use tow truck o

toad

o   o   o

to   to

toad   toad

do   do

dog   dog

t   t

out   out

shout   shout

loud   loud

43

The tow letters always end with a tow.

w is w

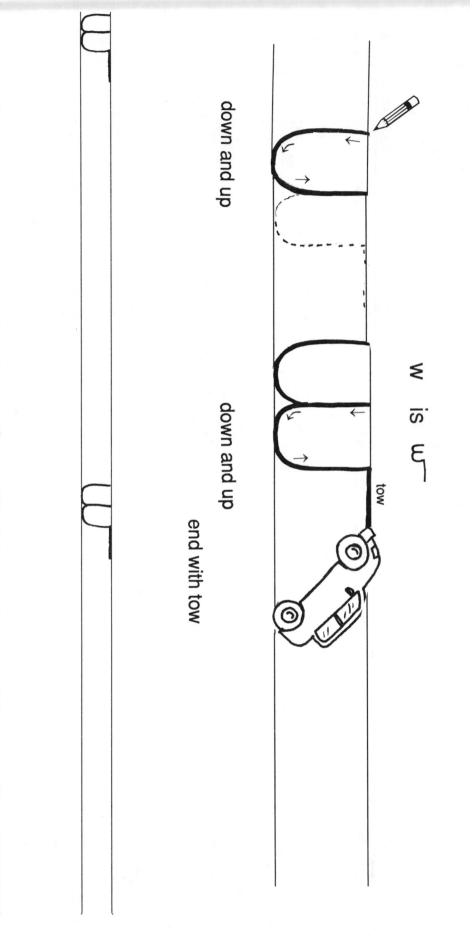

down and up

down and up

end with tow

tow

44

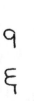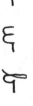

Tow Truck Letters σ w b v
Only four letters have an ending that sticks out.
These letters are made with a "tow."
The next letter must join at the "tow."
For now, always make a "straight across tow."

Now you are ready to use tow truck

saw

from

was

wait

saw

wood

flew

lawyer

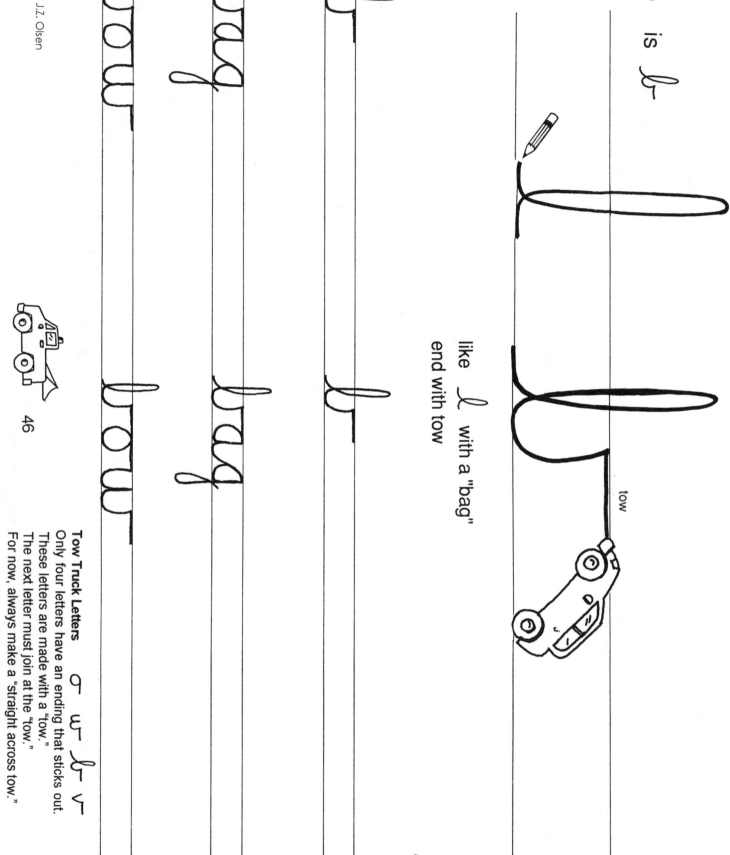

b   is   *b*

like *l* with a "bag"
end with tow

tow

Tow Truck Letters   *o   w   b   v*
Only four letters have an ending that sticks out.
These letters are made with a "tow."
The next letter must join at the "tow."
For now, always make a "straight across tow."

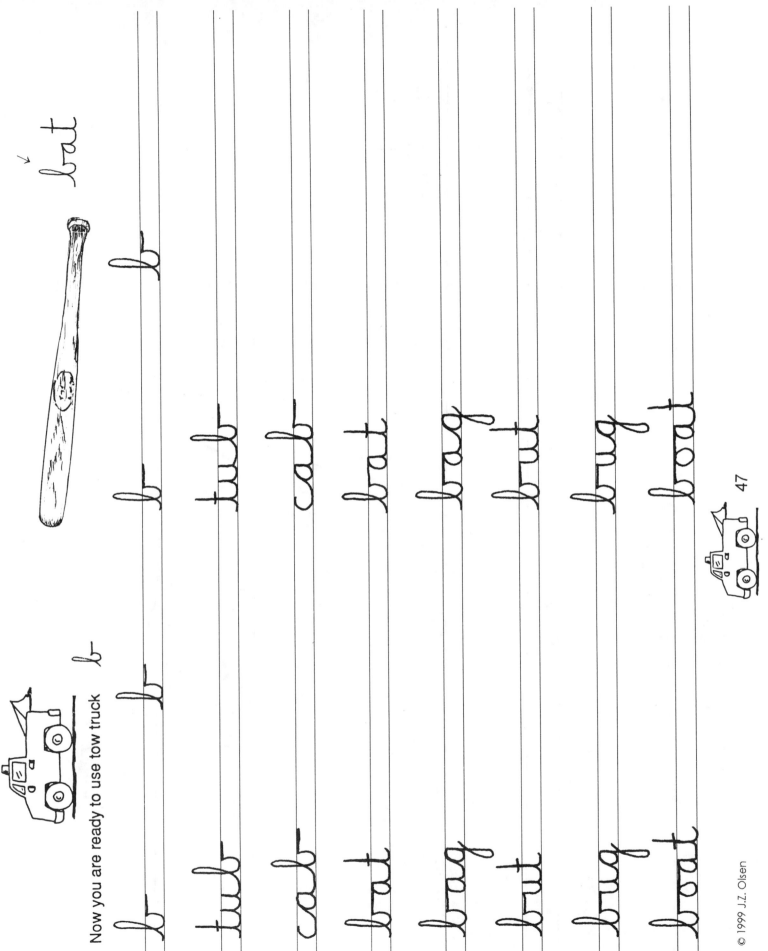

Now you are ready to use tow truck

bat

47

© 1999 J.Z. Olsen

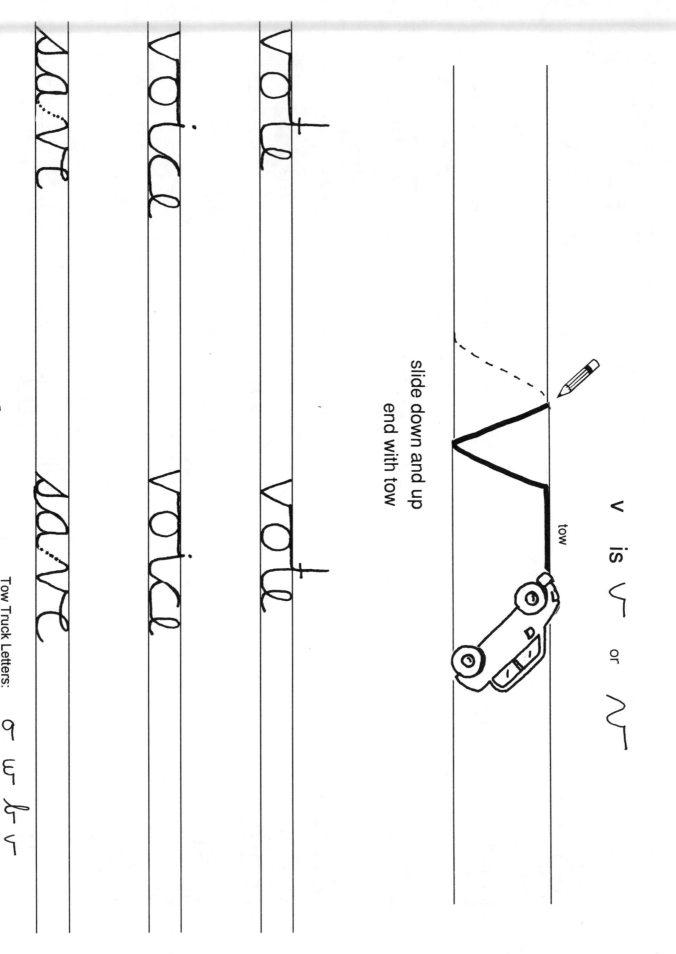

v is ⌄ or ⌄

tow

slide down and up
end with tow

vote

voice

wave

vote

voice

wave

Tow Truck Letters: o w b v

Only four letters have an ending that sticks out.
These letters are made with a "tow."
The next letter must join at the "tow."
For now, always make a "straight across tow."

48

Now you are ready to use tow truck

vase

avocado

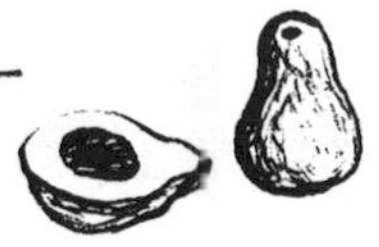

lava

voyage

vase

vocal

voyage

lava

avoid

avocado

vow

V

V

vase

vocal

voyage

lava

avoid

avocado

vow

After a tow truck letter, use:

t   h   k

| | | |

t   cat   hot   not   lot

| | | |

h   who   whale   why   what

| | | |

k   cake   joke   look   cook

Tow Truck Mastery

After a tow truck letter, use:

t   *t*   *t*   *t*

t   *old*   *sold*   *out*   *brout*

t   *sofa*   *off*   *office*

b   *job*   *sob*   *not*   *not*   *hobby*

51

Tow Truck Mastery

Make the tow like a smile!
Here's how to add cursive *i* and cursive *n*.

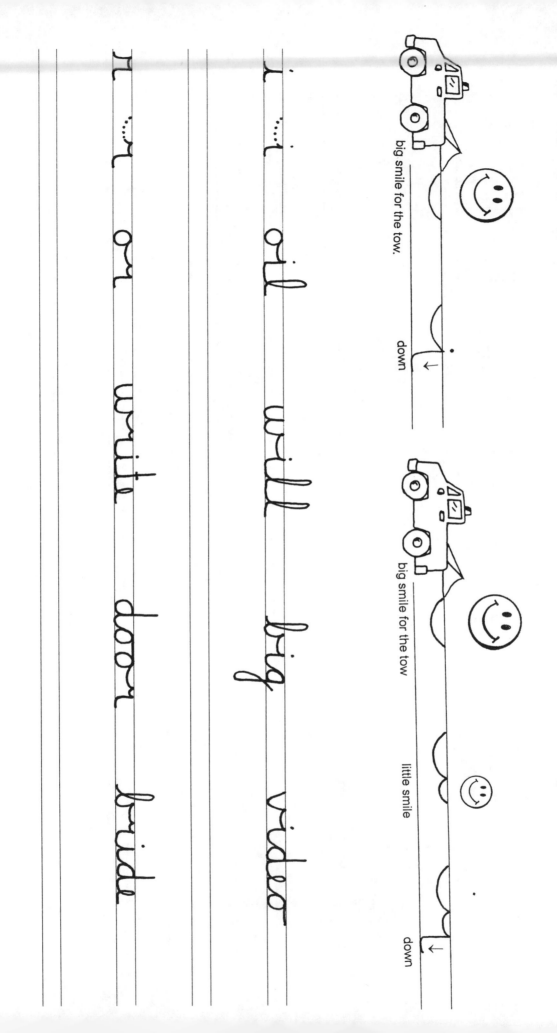

big smile for the tow.   down

big smile for the tow   little smile   down

i   *oil*   *will*   *big*   *video*

i   *on*   *writ*   *door*   *bride*

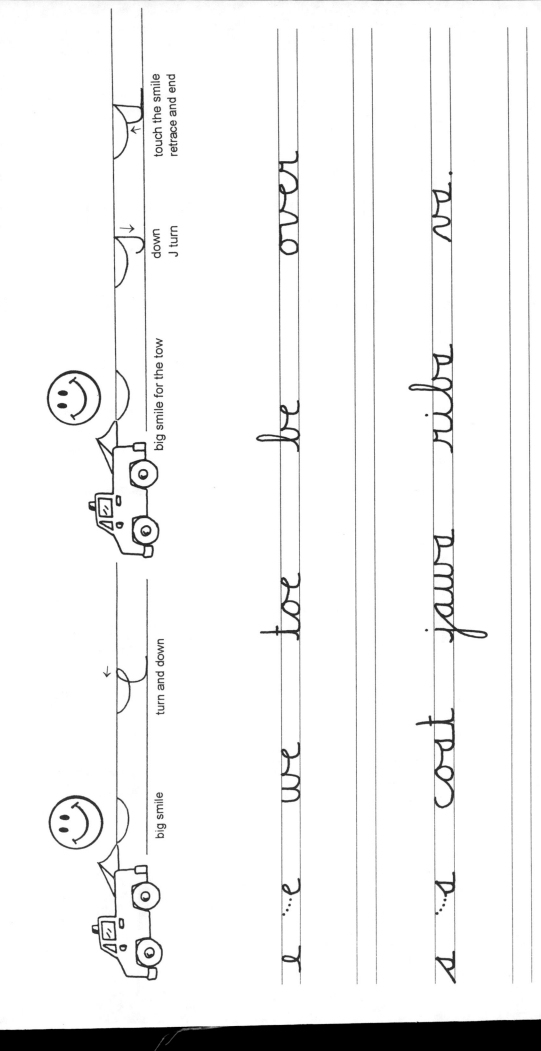

Tow Truck Mastery

Make the tow like a smile!
Here's how to add cursive *l* and cursive *d*.

big smile

turn and down

big smile for the tow

down
J turn

touch the smile
retrace and end

l   *e*   we   toe   over

d   *d*   coat   jaw   ride   we.

1.

2.

3 bumps!

up
over
down

music

m m

me me

my my

time time

make make

music music

him him

them them

© 1999 J.Z. Olsen

55

Special Situation:

It's a mistake to think $\mathcal{m}$ always has 3 bumps. After a tow truck letter, use 2 bumps, just like printed m. It's easy - if you are starting m on the bottom line, use 3 bumps. If you are starting on the top line (where the tow ends!) use printed m (2 bumps). m

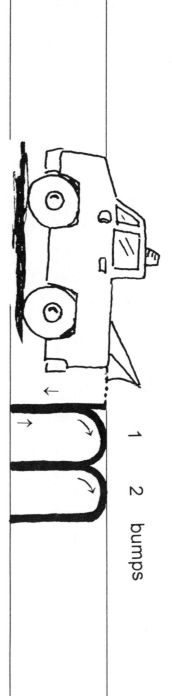

1   2   bumps

Don't forget me!   Oh yes! After any tow truck letter, you must use **printed m.**

56

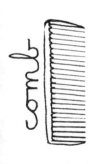

comb

m   m   m

comb   comb

home   home

room   room

from   from

promise   promise

some   some

omit   omit

57

n is m

up
over
down

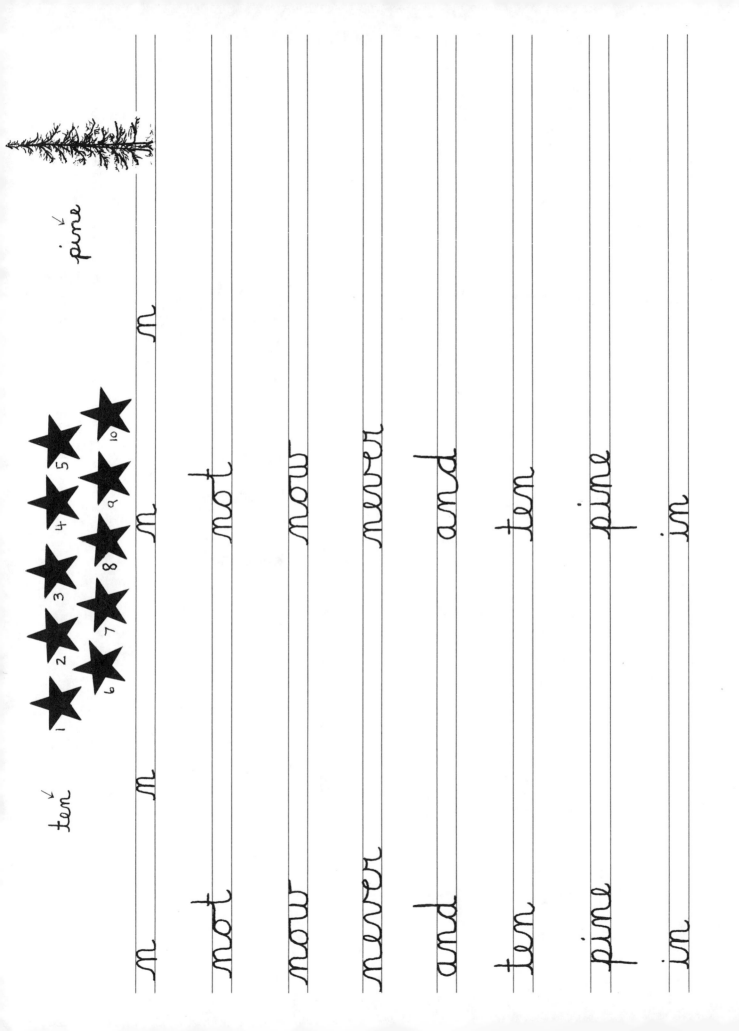

ten

pine

n

not

now

never

and

ten

pine

in

Special Situation:

It's a mistake to think $\cap$ always has 2 bumps. After a tow truck letter, use 1 bump, just like printed n. It's easy - if you are starting n on the bottom line, use 2 bumps. If you are starting on the top line (where the tow ends!) use printed n (1 bump). n

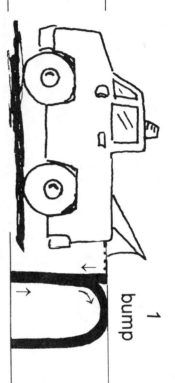

1
bump

Don't forget me!

Oh yes! After any tow truck letter, you must use **printed n.**

n

n

on

On

onl

onl

© 1999 J.Z. Olsen

60

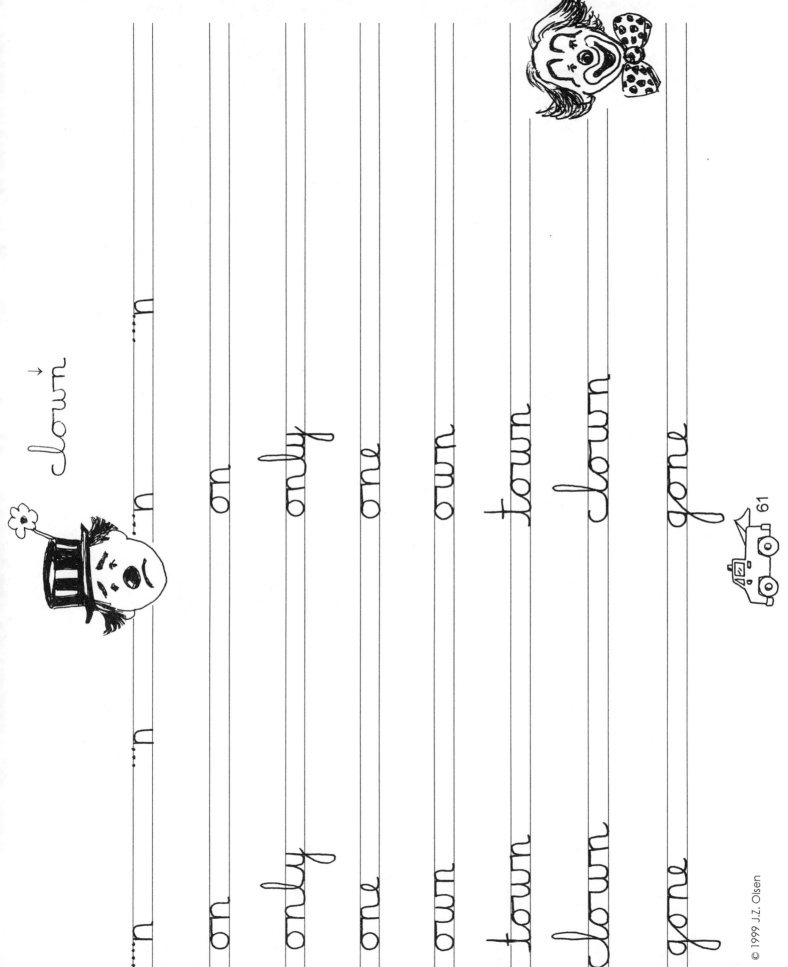

clown

n   n

on   on

only   only

one   one

own   own

town   town

down   down

gone   gone

61

After a tow truck letter use —

1. slide down
2. cross

tow

climb up first, then
1. slide down
2. cross

tow

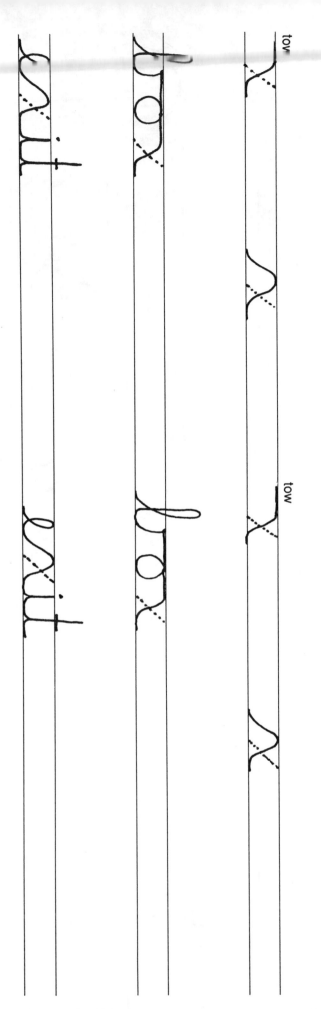

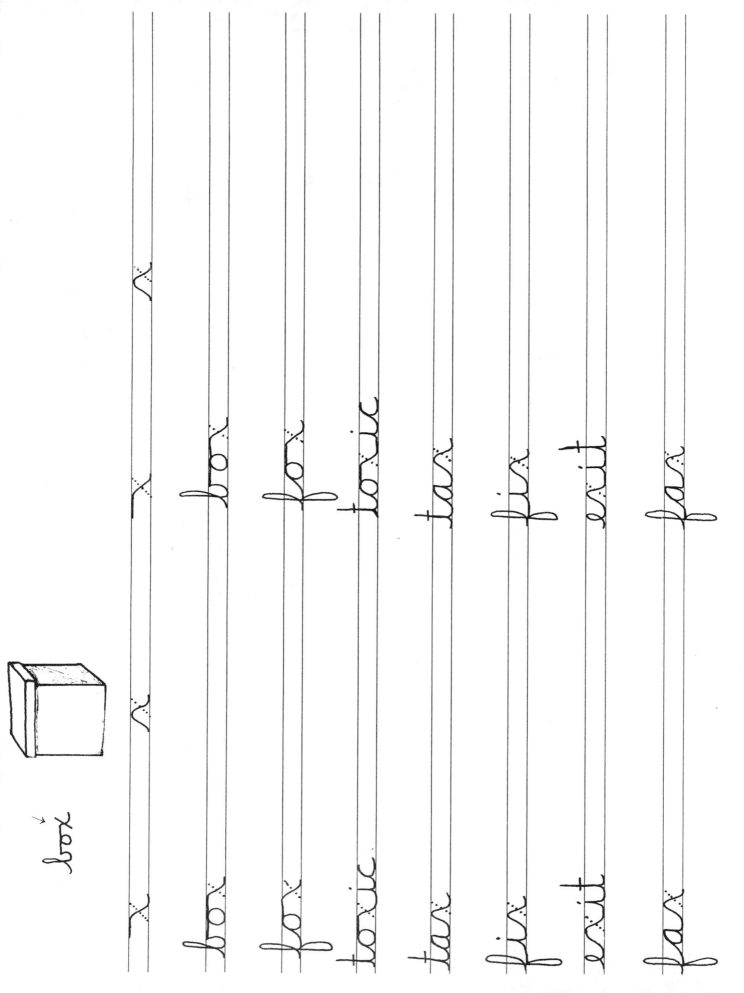

a b c d e f g h i j k l m n

han then when – taking making

ink pink think – sank tank hank

extra extreme expect – seed weed feed

me mean jeans – rain train brain

p r s t u v w x y

tax fax - happy happen

fix six sixty - man more many

node rose chose - have save wave

nest rest best - on ant want

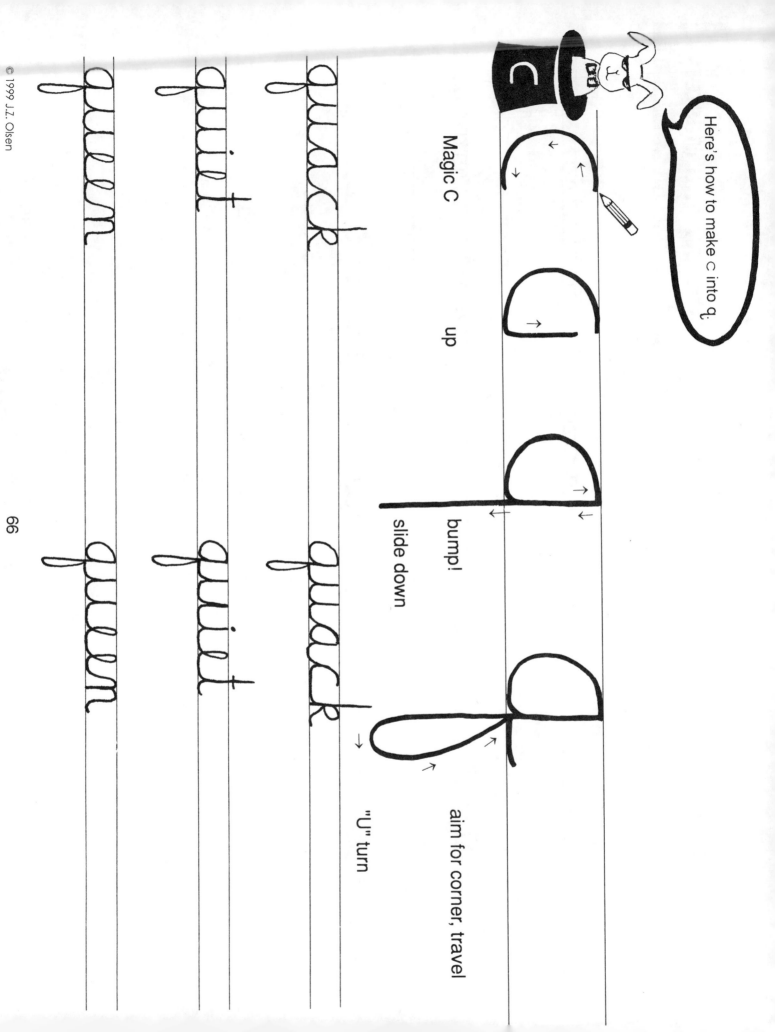

Here's how to make c into q.

Magic C

up

bump!

slide down

aim for corner, travel

"U" turn

quack

quit

quun

quack

quit

quun

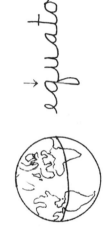

equator

q   q   q

quick   quick

quote   quote

equator   equator

equal   equal

quarter   quarter

quiet   quiet

quarrel   quarrel

My half

Make your half

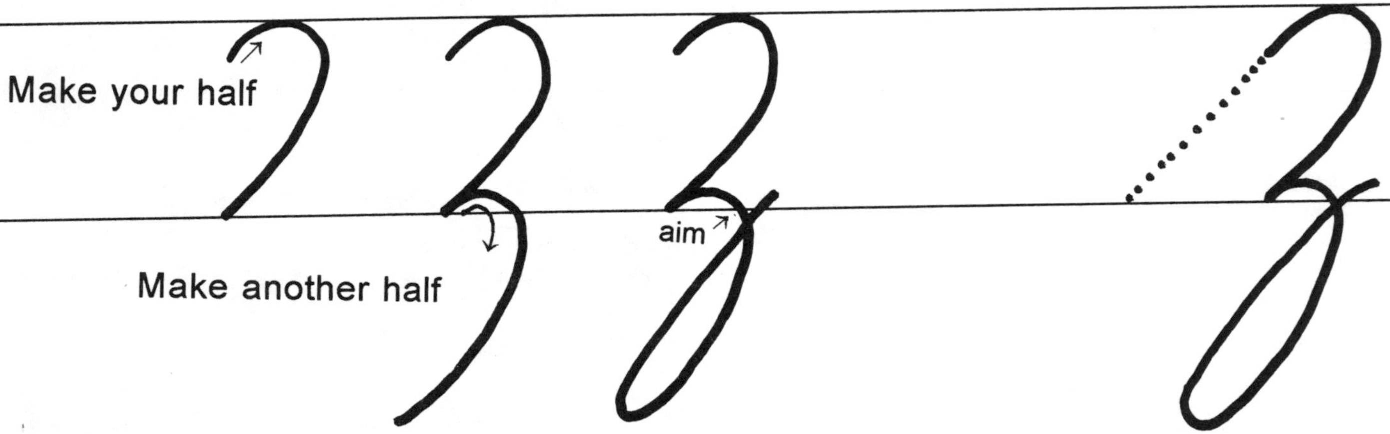

Make your half

Make another half

aim

zoo

zip

lazy

zoo

zip

lazy

68

zero 0123 pizza jazz

Louis Armstrong

z Z

zip

zoom

zero

zap

size

pizza

jazz

69

Let's Learn Capitals!

Capitalize the first word in every sentence.

Here are three famous towers.

Capitalize the pronoun I.
Capitalize titles (Mrs., Mr., Dr., Ms., President, etc...) that are used before a person's name.
Capitalize initials.

" I have a dream... , said Dr. Martin L. King, Jr.

Capitalize the beginning of quotations.
Capitalize proper nouns. Proper nouns are names of specific people, places or things.

Billy said, " Miami, New York City and Austin "

Capitalize the first, last, and other important words in titles of books, movies, plays, music, poems, and works of art.

Sarah, Plain and Tall is a book.

Thanks to Edith H. Fine, co-author of Nitty Gritty Grammar.

Venice, Italy

Aa Cc Oo Uu Vv Ww Xx Yy Zz

You can use these cursive capitals right away. They are like the lower case, but larger.

Chunks of ice float in the Arctic Ocean.

Women won the right to vote in Wyoming.

You won't find cars in Venice or on Venus.

Zebras live in Africa. Unicorns live in myths.

71

That's how to start all these letters - cursive P R B N M

Ready | **set** | **up and over**

P R B N M
P R B n m

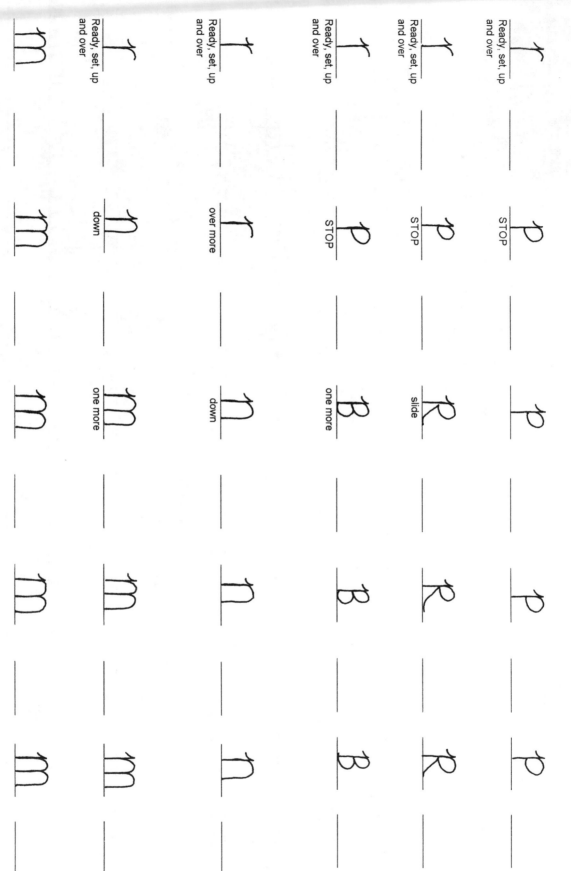

Ready, set, up
and over
P — STOP | P | P

Ready, set, up
and over
P — STOP | R | R

Ready, set, up
and over
P — STOP | B — one more | B

Ready, set, up
and over
r — over more | n — down | n

Ready, set, up
down
n — one more | m | m

Ready, set, up
and over
m | m | m

72

Paul Revere

P R B N M
P R B n m

Mrs. Poe asked for examples of proper nouns.

Billy said, "Miami, New York City and Austin."

Maria said, "Canada, Mexico and Brazil."

Nathan said, "Betsy Ross and Paul Revere."

73

That's how to start T and F in cursive.

Ready　set　J turn

T　F　H　E

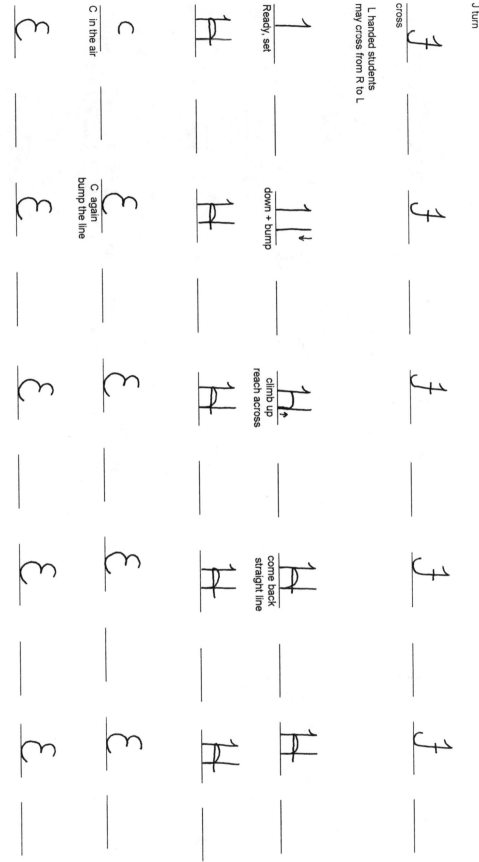
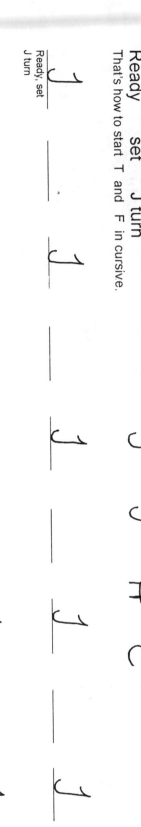
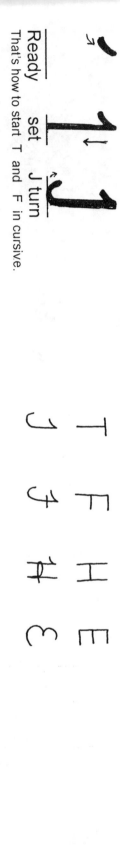

Ready, set
J turn

cross

L handed students
may cross from R to L

Ready, set

down + bump

climb up
reach across

come back
straight line

C in the air

C again
bump the line

T F H E

T F H E

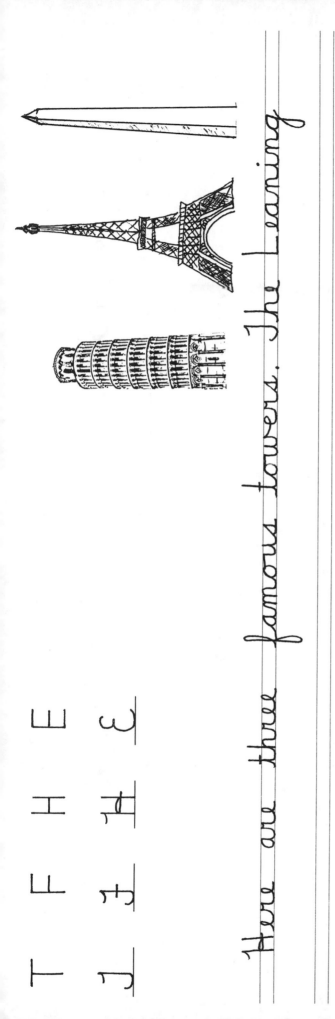

Here are three famous towers. The Leaning

Tower of Pisa is a bell tower. Everyone in

Paris, France knows the Eiffel Tower. The

Washington Monument closed for repairs.

Old Mac Donald had a farm

For cursive G - , think of at the top.

G S D

To end - Stop! Come straight back.

curve up | ℓ part | i part | down - bump | turn | end

no dot!

jet take off | think S

down | tiny J turn | flip over | bump | curl up | end

G S D
A s B

Use capitals for titles. Sarah, Plain and Tall

is a book. Shiloh and Hondy are movies.

"Girls Can Too!" and "Grandfather's Clock" are poems.

"Dusty Old Dust" and "Shenandoah" are songs.

77

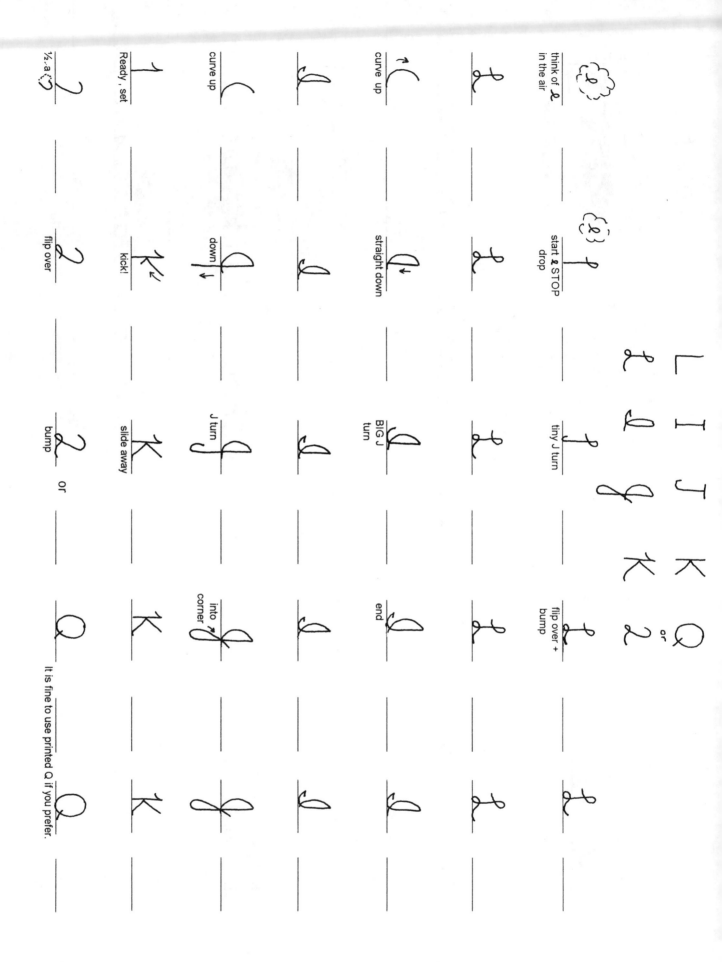

L I J K Q

l i j k q

Mona Lisa

the Mona Lisa, by Leonardo, is in the Louvre.

"I have a dream...," said Dr. Martin L. King, Jr.

Johnny Appleseed's real name was John Chapman.

Queen Victoria and Queen Elizabeth II are related.

79

You need head room for your capital letters!

When you copy these capitals, begin below the top line.

Suggested Pencil Grip and Posture for Right Handed Students

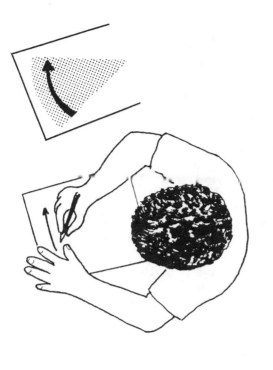

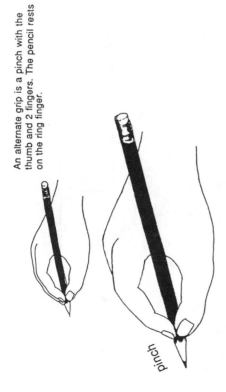

An alternate grip is a pinch with the thumb and 2 fingers. The pencil rests on the ring finger.

The pencil is "pinched" between the thumb pad and the index finger pad. The pencil rests on the middle finger.

pinch

Suggested Pencil Grip and Posture for Left Handed Students

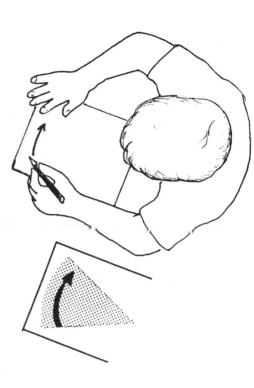

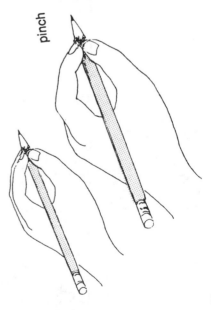

pinch

Aa Bb Cc Dd Ee Ff Gg Hh Ii Jj Kk Ll Mm

Nn Oo Pp Qq Rr Ss Tt Uu Vv Ww Xx Yy Zz

Aa Bb Cc Dd Ee Ff Gg Hh Ii Jj Kk Ll Mm

Nn Oo Pp Qq Rr Ss Tt Uu Vv Ww Xx Yy Zz

Aa Bb Cc Dd Ee Ff Gg Hh Ii Jj Kk Ll Mm

Nn Oo Pp Qq Rr Ss Tt Uu Vv Ww Xx Yy Zz

1 _____

2 _____

3 _____

4 _____

5 _____

6 _____

7 _____

8 _____

9 _____

10 _____

11 _____

12 _____